SHAMBHALA
CLASSICS

Morihei Ueshiba (1883–1969),
Prophet of the Art of Peace.
The photograph is signed
"Ueshiba Morihei" and stamped
with the seal of the Aiki Jinja (shrine).

The Art
of Peace

Morihei Ueshiba

TRANSLATED AND EDITED BY
JOHN STEVENS

SHAMBHALA
Boston & London
2002

Shambhala Publications, Inc.
Horticultural Hall
300 Massachusetts Avenue
Boston, Massachusetts 02115
www.shambhala.com

The author wishes to thank the Ueshiba family for permission to
quote from collections of Morihei's talks and writings, and permission to reproduce images of his calligraphy. Special thanks to
Seiseki Abe for permission to reproduce the images on pages 85
("Ki") and 93 ("Aiki okami"), and to Bay Marin Aikido for the
image on page 88 ("Masakatsu").

13 12 11 10 9 8 7 6 5

Printed in the United States of America

∞ This edition is printed on acid-free paper that meets the
American National Standards Institute Z39.48 Standard.

Distributed in the United States by Random House, Inc.,
and in Canada by Random House of Canada Ltd

Library of Congress Cataloging-in-Publication Data
Ueshiba, Morihei, 1883–1969.
The art of peace/Morihei Ueshiba; translated and edited
by John Stevens.
p. cm.—(Shambhala classics)
"An expanded version"—Pref.
ISBN-13 978-1-57062-964-8
ISBN-10 1-57062-964-1
1. Ueshiba, Morihei, 1883–1969—Teachings. 2. Aikido—
Philosophy. 3. Conflict management. I. Stevens, John, 1947–
II. Title. III. Series.
GV1114.35.U39 2002
796.815′4—dc21
2002005563

CONTENTS

PREFACE

THIS SHAMBHALA CLASSICS EDITION of *The Art of Peace* is an expanded version of the Shambhala pocket edition. I am extremely gratified by, and grateful for, the wide popularity of the pocket edition of *The Art of Peace*. It is likely the best-selling of all Aikido books and has been translated into many languages. As I wrote in that edition, "Morihei Ueshiba, the founder of Aikido, taught the Art of Peace as a creative mind-body discipline, as a practical means of handling aggression, and as a way of life that fosters fearlessness, wisdom, love, and friendship. The master interpreted the Art of Peace in the broadest possible sense and believed that its principles of reconciliation, harmony, cooperation, and empathy could be applied bravely to all the challenges we face in life—in personal relations, in our interactions with other human beings in society, at work, and in business, and when dealing with nature. Everyone can be a warrior for peace." Morihei Ueshiba called his grand vision *Takemusu Aiki*, or "Courageous and Creative Living."

For this edition, there is Part One, which discusses Morihei Ueshiba's life as a prophet of peace; Part Two, which presents his views on the art of war versus the art of peace; and Part Three, "The Art of Peace," Morihei's collected sayings.

Japanese names are presented in Western style, family name last, but I have followed the Japanese practice of referring to revered figures such as Morihei Ueshiba, Kumagusu Minakata, Sokaku Takeda, Onisaburo Deguchi, and Tesshu Yamaoka by their first names. In a few direct quotes, Morihei is referred to as "Ueshiba Sensei," with *sensei* meaning "teacher," or, in this case, "master." The term *ki* (*ch'i* in Chinese) refers to the subtle energy that propels the universe, the vitality that pervades creation, and the unifying force that holds things together. Additionally, the text for this edition has been revised slightly and more quotations have been added. The quotes have been gathered from the corpus of written literature and the vast oral tradition. Other than *doka*, didactic "poems of the Way," Morihei wrote very little himself. This is typically the case for truly great masters, who refrain from setting their teachings in stone, preferring to speak to the moment. It was up to their disciples to listen carefully, discern what the master was saying, and then pass it on. The oral tradition includes tape recordings of Morihei speaking, transcripts of his talks and interviews, and sayings as recalled and collected by his many students, supporters, and admirers. The text is illustrated with examples of Morihei's delightful and inspiring calligraphy.

Although I have been studying the sayings of Morihei Ueshiba for more than thirty years, I was delighted at how many new revelations I had while working on this expanded version, and I was encouraged that I am still so inspired by the original text. I hope readers of this Shambhala Classics Edition of *The Art of Peace* will have the same experience.

—*John Stevens*
Sendai, April 26, 2002

盛平

Morihei's signature.
His name means
"Abundant Peace."

PART ONE

MORIHEI UESHIBA,
PROPHET *of the*
ART *of* PEACE

MORIHEI UESHIBA was born on December 14, 1883, in the city of Tanabe. Tanabe is located on the seacoast of the ancient Kii District (now known as Wakayama Prefecture). The district is famed for its natural beauty—vast mountain ranges, enthralling forests, magnificent waterfalls, hundreds of healing hot springs, lush orchards, and the lovely Inland Sea. It is also home to the grand shrines and temples of Kumano—the sacred space where the Shinto gods descended to earth and where the gateway to Amida Buddha's Pure Land lies hidden—and to Mount Koya, center of Shingon, the Tantric Buddhism of Japan. The district is called "The place where the gods and nature are one." Although Morihei lived most of his adult life away from Wakayama, he returned to the area frequently, and maintained, "No matter where I am, I will always be a child of Kumano at heart." Morihei's father, Yoroku, was a prosperous landowner and longtime town councilman, and his mother Yuki was related to the Takeda clan, one of the greatest of the old *samurai* families. Morihei was their only son (they had four daughters), and they considered him a gift from the gods.

Morihei, born a bit prematurely, was rather frail and sickly as a child but grew into a robust teenager, thanks to a steady diet of outdoor exercise—swimming and fishing in the bay in spring and summer, and hiking in the mountains in fall and winter—and sumo wrestling.

The people of Kumano are very pious. From age five, Morihei rose at 4:00 A.M. to accompany his mother to her daily worship of the local gods. Morihei spent much of his youth engaged in pilgrimages to mountain shrines and temples and in practicing *misogi*, ritual Shinto purification in waterfalls and in the ocean. Morihei was captivated by tales told of local wizards such as En no Gyoja, the first *yamabushi* (mountain ascetic), and he never tired of hearing of the miracles performed by wonder workers like the Buddhist saint Kukai, the founder of the Shingon monastery on Mount Koya. From an early age Morihei himself had mystical experiences. For instance, once a pitch-dark mountain path he was walking on suddenly became illumined by an eerie light; another time he had an instantaneous sensation of feeling light as a bird soaring high above the peaks.

Morihei was sent to a temple school to learn the weighty Confucian classics, but he far preferred participation in the spectacular esoteric rites of Shingon Buddhism. He valued exoteric science as well, devouring hundreds of books on mathematics, chemistry, and physics. Morihei loved to study, but he did not like being cooped up in a classroom and left school at age fourteen. He did graduate from an abacus academy, though, and took a job at the local tax office. However, this type of office work did not really interest him; (plus, he often sided with the taxpayers against the government). In 1901, with the support of his father and some rich relatives, eighteen-year-old Morihei ventured to the capital city of Tokyo to seek his fortune. He did well, establishing a thriving stationery business there, but city life was not for him. Morihei turned over the entire business to his employees and returned, empty-handed, to Tanabe within a year. During his stay in Tokyo, he received his first training in *bujutsu*, the traditional martial arts of Japan, and he also did some Zen meditation at a temple in Kamakura.

In October of 1902, Morihei married Hatsu Itogawa. In 1903, Morihei joined an army regiment based in Wakayama. War was brewing between Japan and Russia, and full-scale fighting seemed imminent. Fiercely competitive and driven to compensate for his small stature—Morihei was only 1.56 meters tall, less than the minimum requirement for military service, causing him to fail his initial induction physical exam—Morihei became an extraordinarily gung-ho soldier when he was finally allowed to join the army: out-marching, out-shooting, and out-drilling all the other members of his regiment. War did break out between Japan and Russia in 1904, and Morihei was sent to the Manchurian Front in 1905. Morihei was kept away from the main battlefields because he was his family's only son, but he was assigned to the military police and saw action against Chinese bandits. The war ended quickly (albeit with much bloodshed on both sides) in 1905, in Japan's favor. Morihei was then offered a place in the Military Officers Training School but turned it down. Morihei said later, "I enjoyed being in the military when I was a young man, but even then I innately felt that war is never the solution to any problem. War always brings death and destruction and that can never be a good thing." He was discharged from the army in 1906 and returned to Tanabe to farm and fish.

After his discharge, Morihei seemed to be at a loss regarding his future. He began to act strangely, shutting himself up in his room or suddenly disappearing into the mountains. However, Morihei did continue his practice of Japanese martial arts—his father even built a *dojo* (training hall) on the family property for him and engaged a *judo* teacher for private instruction. Morihei studied other martial arts as well and eventually received a *yagyu ryu jujutsu* certificate in 1908.

In 1909, Morihei came under the beneficial influence of the eccentric Kumagusu Minakata (1867–1941), who had settled in Tanabe following many years abroad. Although Kumagusu was one of the greatest scholars Japan had ever produced—he was said to have had commanded a dozen languages and wrote hundreds of research papers on an enormous variety of subjects—like Morihei, he spent hardly any time in a classroom. His erudition was due to a prodigious, photographic memory and unending research. Kumagusu once declared, "I want to know everything; my curiosity is boundless." Kumagusu opened a

people's university in Tanabe, and in his teaching he emphasized the comparability, compatibility, and interrelatedness of
the Japanese and other peoples of the world, not their unique-
ness. He was also an intense social activist and environmen-
talist who taught Morihei to oppose injustice and protect the
environment. Morihei did not get any pacifist ideas from Kumagusu, who was expelled from the British Museum for slug-
ging a fellow researcher because of a racist remark, but he was
inspired by Kumagusu's wide learning, his international vision,
and his willingness to accept any challenge.

Looking for new worlds to conquer, in 1912 Morihei led a
group of settlers from Tanabe to the wilds of Hokkaido, Japan's
northernmost, largely undeveloped island. The group settled
in remote Shirataki, and started to build a village from scratch.
Morihei worked tirelessly to make the project a success. He
put up buildings; cleared the land for the cultivation of pota-
toes, peppermint, and sesame; engaged in prudent logging of
the great forests; raised horses; and eventually served as a local
councilman. (Despite Morihei's great efforts, the settlement
never really succeeded. Crops failed the first few years, and
there was a disastrous fire in 1916 that destroyed 80 percent of
the village, including Morihei's first home. Morihei did learn
how to tame wild animals, though, becoming pals with several
big Hokkaido bears.)

In 1915, Morihei encountered awesome Sokaku Takeda
(1859–1943), the grand master of *daito ryu aiki jutsu*. Sokaku
epitomized the last generation of old-time warriors. Born in
Aizu (located in present-day Fukushima Prefecture), home of
the fiercest samurai in Japan, Sokaku was given instruction in
lethal martial arts as soon as he could walk. His youth was devoted to traveling all over Japan to train with the best martial
art masters and to taking on all comers in street fights. He
killed several thugs in a fight when he was fifteen, and when he
was twenty-two he took on forty construction workers in a

brawl that become known as the Nihonmatsu Incident (after the town where it occurred). He cut down eight or nine workers and injured many others. Although badly wounded himself in the battle, Sokaku managed to escape. He was exonerated by the authorities, who accepted his plea of self-defense, but they made him put away his sword. (Even without a live blade, Sokaku still managed to wreak havoc on foolhardy challengers, and later dispatched one such foe with a bamboo sword.)

After this incident, Sokaku disappeared for a number of years. Even after he surfaced again in 1898, as a teacher of *daito ryu aiki jutsu*, he kept constantly on the move—not surprisingly since he had many enemies who had sworn to get revenge. He traveled with a walking stick containing a hidden blade, and he concealed an unsheathed knife in his kimono. Sokaku would not enter a building, even his own house, without first calling out and waiting until someone he recognized appeared to escort him in, and he would not take any food or drink until it had been tested for poison.

Although tiny and thin, Sokaku was a peerless martial artist who was in great demand as an instructor. Sokaku conducted seminars for police officials, military men, and aristocrats all over northern Japan and Hokkaido, and it was at one such seminar that Morihei was introduced to him. Easily defeated by the gremlin *daito ryu* master, Morihei become Sokaku's student and trained intensely under his harsh tutelage.

The martial techniques that Sokaku taught Morihei were very effective, since they were, in fact, derived from years of actual combat, in fights to the death. Sokaku was an amazingly creative fighter. Once in an altercation with a bunch of construction workers, he leaped to the top of a dike they were building and collapsed a portion of it, trapping his adversaries in the mud. Another time, when he was ambushed in a public bath by a bunch of hooligans trying to catch him with his pants down, Sokaku turned his wet bath towel into a weapon, stunning his attackers with sharp cracks across their eyes and hard blows to their ribs and genitals. Also, it seems that Sokaku had Morihei act as his "proxy" on occasion, sending him out to deal with assassins looking for the *daito ryu* master. This gave Morihei first hand experience in dealing with a murderous attack. (It should be said, however, that even though Sokaku was unrivaled as a street fighter, he still maintained the secret of the martial arts as: "Hear the soundless sound, and see the formless form. At a glance, read your opponent's mind, and attain victory without contention.")

In addition to his training, Morihei had acquired tremendous strength from years of strenuous physical labor wrestling huge logs and from the hard and heavy work of pioneering (which included dealing with violent gangsters and escaped criminals who thrived on the largely lawless frontier). Yet he still felt restless and unfulfilled, both as a martial artist and as a human being. When news arrived of his father's grave illness back in Tanabe, Morihei immediately turned over all of his property to Sokaku and left Hokkaido for good in 1919, after a sojourn of seven years.

On the way back home, Morihei made an impetuous detour to visit the headquarters of the Omoto-kyo religion, located in Ayabe, to pray for his father's recovery. There, Morihei had another momentous encounter, this time with enigmatic Onisaburo Deguchi (1871–1947). A few months after his father's death—Yoroku had died before Morihei was able to get back to Tanabe, just as Onisaburo had predicted—Morihei became the disciple of Onisaburo, and in 1920 he moved his family to the Omoto-kyo compound in Ayabe.

Omoto-kyo had been founded by Nao Deguchi (1836–1918), a wretchedly poor peasant woman who became possessed by the god Konjin in 1892 and then began prophesizing in that deity's name: "Do away with emperors, kings, and artificial government; establish true equality; abolish capitalism; live in

God's heart, simply and purely!" Later, Onisaburo, who had married Nao's daughter Sumi, became the chief spokesman of the religion. Omoto-kyo was an eclectic, mystical religion that emphasized the harmony of all creeds, social justice, natural farming, and practice of the fine and applied arts. It was pacifist in orientation—Onisaburo said, "There is nothing in the world more harmful than war and more foolish than armament." The brilliant, charismatic, flamboyant, and clairvoyant Onisaburo was the first person to perceive the true purpose of Morihei's life: "Your mission on earth is to become a prophet of peace, to teach the world the real meaning of *budo* ("Way of Martial Valor").

Morihei's first year in Ayabe was not auspicious. He and his wife lost two infant sons to illness: Takemori, aged three, and Kuniharu, who only lived one month. (They had two other children: their daughter, Matsuko, was born in 1911, and their son, Kisshomaru, was born in 1921.) A much happier event was the opening of Morihei's first training hall on the grounds of the Omoto-kyo compound. Sokaku visited Ayabe in 1922 and stayed for six months giving instruction, but the situation was tense throughout his entire visit. Onisaburo took one look at Sokaku and pronounced, "The man reeks of blood and violence." Onisaburo encouraged Morihei to establish his own path, and Morihei began distancing himself from Sokaku and the *daito ryu*. (By 1936, Morihei and Sokaku had completely parted ways.)

One day at the Omoto-kyo compound, a construction crew of ten men tried to reposition a large tree, but they were unable to do so because of their dissension regarding the best procedure. Morihei appeared on the scene and was suddenly angered. "Why can't people cooperate better? Why is there so much contention in our world?" Thus agitated, Morihei grabbed the tree and single-handedly moved it to its new location. Onisaburo happened to be present as well and said to Morihei, "That is the power of righteous indignation. Channel that tremendous force into the proper activity and you will accomplish wonderful things."

Onisaburo was not a martial artist himself, but he did on occasion practice *kyudo*, classical Japanese archery, shooting arrows tipped with prayers of peace and love, and he possessed a secret technique called *aiki-kiri* (cleaving with a cut of the spirit). Onisaburo and Morihei would sometimes spend an entire night secluded in a thicket, cutting bamboo with their bare hands using that technique, which Onisaburo imparted only to Morihei.

In 1924, Onisaburo, Morihei, and several other Omoto-kyo members embarked on "The Great Mongolian Adventure," hoping to locate Shambhala and establish a heaven on earth. This quixotic quest was symbolic of Onisaburo's incurable optimism and unshakable faith in himself and his mission. The group survived floods, hailstorms, near starvation, poisoned food, attacks by bandits, and capture by a Chinese army. They were sentenced to death and led to the execution ground, only to be saved by a last-minute reprieve. Even after they were sent back to Japan, the mission a seeming failure, Onisaburo was unfazed— "Better luck next time," he remarked, and went on to plan still greater schemes.

Morihei, however, was forever changed by the many extreme, face-to-face encounters with death he experienced during the adventure. He had been thrown through the windshield of the group's vehicle when it crashed and was badly cut; he had engaged in deadly hand-to-hand combat with cutthroat highwaymen; he exchanged gunfire with a Chinese militia; and he had been placed in chains and taken, through a field strewn with freshly executed corpses, to face a firing squad. In particular, he was affected by this experience:

> As we neared Tungliao, we were trapped in a valley and showered with bullets. Miraculously, I could sense the di-

rection of the projectiles—beams of light indicated their paths of flight—and I was able to dodge the bullets. The ability to sense an attack is what the ancient masters meant by anticipation. If one's mind is steady and pure, one can instantly perceive an attack and avoid it—that, I realized, is the essence of *aiki* (the art of harmonization).

Morihei returned to Ayabe a different person. He intensified his training, and in the spring of 1925, his life was transformed and his mission made clear. After meeting a challenge made by a *kendo* master—the swordsman gave up in defeat after failing to land a single blow—Morihei walked out into his garden to wipe the perspiration from his face.

Suddenly the earth trembled. Golden vapor welled up from the ground and engulfed me. I felt transformed into a golden image, and my body seemed as light as a feather. I could understand the speech of the birds. All at once I understood the nature of creation: the Way of a Warrior is to manifest divine love, a spirit that embraces and nurtures all things. Tears of gratitude and joy streamed down my cheeks. I saw the entire earth as my home, and the sun, moon, and stars as my intimate friends. All attachment to material things vanished.

"I am the universe!" Morihei proclaimed; he felt that he had been summoned to serve as a messenger for Miroku Bosatsu, the golden buddha-to-come, who will bring heaven down to earth. After this dramatic enlightenment experience, Morihei became an invincible warrior and set off on his mission as a prophet of the Art of Peace.

A revealing tale illuminates Morihei's transformation from material to spiritual warrior. In Tanabe, there was a man named Suzuki who had regularly defeated Morihei when they were young *judo* students. Later, when Morihei returned to Tanabe after learning *daito ryu aiki jutsu* in Hokkaido, he and Suzuki had another contest; Morihei was injured so badly attempting a throw that he had to spend a month in bed. However, after Morihei's revelation in Ayabe, Suzuki was no match for Morihei and became his student.

Following his spiritual awakening, Morihei acquired the reputation as "Master of Masters." In 1927, he moved to Tokyo at the request of many influential patrons, and then opened a permanent *dojo* in 1931. In the old days, it was not at all uncommon for a challenger to be maimed or killed when he was defeated by a master (such as Sokaku, who was forever boasting of the number of men he had done in). Morihei, in sharp contrast, handled any kind of attack without causing serious injury to his opponent. (Early in his teaching career, Morihei had hurt a fiercely resisting opponent rather badly, and he thereafter resolved to refine his technique to allow his partners to escape injury. Another challenger had been severely harmed when he missed Morihei and, unable to stop his momentum, crashed into a wall, so Morihei instructed his students to learn to take safe breakfalls "like a cat.") A famous *judo* competitor named Nishimura went after Morihei repeatedly but kept ending up on the mat, unable to figure out how he got there. Exhausted, Nishimura looked up from the ground at the smiling Morihei and wondered, "Can there really be a martial art in which one downs his attacker with a smile?" After such an initiation, most people immediately petitioned Morihei to become his student. He told them, "I like those who are spirited. If you are willing to devote yourself to helping others, to improve the world at large, I will accept you as a student. However, you cannot practice this Path half-heartedly—it is all or nothing."

In other martial arts, masters practice smashing tiles and bricks to turn their hands and feet into weapons of mayhem, but Morihei's blows were devastatingly effective without actually making contact. Rinjiro Shirata (1912–1993), one of Morihei's earliest students, described how it felt to face off against the master:

When I stood before Ueshiba Sensei, all I could see was his mesmerizing eyes; they seemed to engulf me completely. All of my energy was taken away and I felt powerless. When I tried to strike him, he would counter-strike. While his blow never touched my body, it completely neutralized my attack, dispersed all my power, and broke my concentration so all I could do was crumble. If he threw me, I felt as if I was floating on a cloud, totally swallowed up in his presence. When he pinned you, on the other hand, it was like receiving an electric shock that paralyzed your entire body.

Other students spoke of feeling as if they were being swept up in a windstorm or blinded by a ball of fire when thrown by Morihei; some had the sensation of entering a different dimension, and a few even saw stars when they hit the mat, but then felt remarkably energized. Grabbing Morihei's arm "was like trying to hold on to the trunk of a pine tree," one student said. Another student said that when the master squeezed his wrist, "it was like having a red-hot wire applied to your arm." A student who once did sword-work with Morihei remarked, "His sword was pressed lightly against my thumb, causing only a slightly painful sensation, but he held me completely immobile." Morihei's *kiai*, "spirited shout," was high-pitched; rather than an ear-piercing noise, it was more of an overwhelming vibration that shook an opponent to his core. All challengers reported that there was no sense of resistance or struggle against their attacks—there was literally nothing to grasp or hit.

Many of Morihei's early students were extremely strong, and he had to instruct them not to overdo it. Shirata, for example, would frequently break his partner's wrist by merely twisting it. "Too hard, Shirata," Morihei would admonish him. "Softer, softer!" Shirata would attempt to ease up, but he found himself reverting to pure physical force if his training partner resisted. Morihei said, "Well, you are still young and don't know how to control your own strength yet. Here is my advice: Throw your partner by not throwing, pin him by not pinning." Shirata learned the lesson well. When he was teaching in Morihei's stead in Osaka, Shirata mentioned the key Aikido concept of *muteiko*, "nonresistance." Suddenly, a champion sumo wrestler jumped up from the crowd of onlookers and came at Shirata, shouting, "Nonresist this!" Shirata pinned the wrester to the ground in a flash, and then laughed, "See? No one can resist nonresistance!" (Shirata's rival at the *dojo* was Yukawa Tsutomu [d. 1943], nicknamed the "Kobukan Samson." Tragically, Yukawa was stabbed to death in an altercation in Osaka. When Morihei heard the news, the master said sadly, "What a pity. He was too strong for his own good." People possessing tremendous strength have a very difficult time controlling themselves and easily make enemies.)

Shirata's fellow student Hajime Iwata recalled:

We slept in the *dojo* and often Ueshiba Sensei would suddenly appear in the middle of the night, roust us from our beds, and command us to attack him any way we liked, with all our might. New techniques came to him in his sleep and he wanted to try them out immediately. He was extraordinarily creative and dynamic in those days. He told us that "*Budo* means constant progress, and lifelong training." What lingers in my mind most, however, was his attitude during prayer. It was so respectful, calm, and dignified, whether he was praying before the *dojo* shrine or outdoors where he would simply raise his eyes toward heaven.

Morihei at prayer made a deep impression on all of his disciples. Shirata commented, "I'll never forget how Ueshiba Sensei looked at prayer—his form was so beautiful, so elevating—and that's what inspired me the most throughout the years." Other disciples noted that when Morihei prayed before the Iwama outdoor Aiki Shrine in summer, the swarms of mosquitoes and flies that relentlessly pursued the attendants stayed completely away from the master—his chants kept them at bay. Whenever Morihei visited his home prefecture of Wakayama, he paid a visit to the Kumano Shrine. He would usually perform a special demonstration of Aikido in the open area before the shrine as an offering to the gods. One time his visit occurred during a torrential downpour. Morihei waited a bit under the shrine eaves, and then announced, "I will begin now." The rain suddenly stopped and the sun came out, bathing Morihei in light. When he finished, the rain again came down in buckets.

A professional wrestler from the United States named Mangan came to visit. When he asked to be accepted as student, Morihei told him (through an interpreter), "If you can escape from my pin—and I will only use one finger—I'll accept you. Come and attack me any way you like." The wrestler launched a flying dropkick, missed completely, and was pinned by Morihei as soon as he landed. Even though Mangan could not escape, Morihei still let him train for the duration of his short stay in Japan. The wrestler kept pestering Morihei to come to America, where he "could make millions of dollars in challenge matches."

Morihei's greatest challenge, and the one most significant to his role as prophet of the Art of Peace, was witnessed by Gozo Shioda (1915–1994), another of Morihei's early students:

One day [in the mid-1930's] a group of army sharp-shooters visited the *dojo* to observe a demonstration by Ueshiba Sensei. After the demonstration, Sensei suddenly announced, "Bullets cannot touch me." This was a direct provocation, and the marksmen immediately challenged him to prove it at their home firing range. Sensei agreed and a date was set. Sensei put his fingerprint on a document absolving the marksmen of all responsibility if he was shot and killed. Sensei's wife pleaded with him not to go, and even I, who had witnessed Sensei's amazing feats many times, thought that he was going too far this time—I told another disciple, "Time to start planning Sensei's funeral." Sensei assured all of us: "Do not worry. They will never be able to hit me." He proceeded to the firing range in a surprisingly light-hearted mood. When we reached the firing range, we found that not one but six marksmen would be taking aim at Sensei. As Sensei positioned himself as a human target, twenty-five meters from the firing line, I wondered how he could possibly escape from that distance against so many shooters. "Ready, aim, fire!" went the command. There was a loud explosion, a swirl of smoke, and suddenly one of the marksmen went flying. Morihei was standing behind the shooters, laughing. All of us were totally stunned and bewildered. We asked him to perform the miracle again, and he agreed. The scene was repeated—the shots, the explosion of noise and smoke, a flying marksman, and Sensei standing behind the shooters. Even though I had tried to keep my eyes glued on Sensei's form, I could not discern anything. On the way home, I asked him, "How did you do that?" He told me: "The actual bullets are preceded by a golden beam of light. Although they seem to fire in unison, there is always one bullet that is first, and that is the beam of light I avoided. I then leaped *ninja* style to bridge the distance and throw the marksman who had fired the first shot." Then he added, cryptically, "In truth, my purpose on earth is not fully accomplished yet so nothing can harm me. Once my task is completed, then it will be time to go, but until then I'm perfectly safe." This is how he explained it to me, but quite honestly I still cannot understand what he did that day.

Through this instructive tale, Morihei shows us that the spiritual can defeat the material, even against the most overwhelming, seemingly impossible, odds. Armed with modern and efficient weapons of destruction, the arrogant military marksmen were still no match for one who was functioning on a higher, more spiritual level. It also shows that Morihei was well aware that he had a definite mission as prophet of the Art of Peace. (The Japanese word I have translated as "prophet" is *amakudaru*, which also means "incarnation" and "avatar." Morihei often used that term when referring to himself.)

The war years from 1931 (date of the Manchurian Incident in China, which Onisaburo called "the beginning of hell") to 1945 were very trying for Morihei. His guru Onisaburo was thrown into jail in 1935 by a government afraid of his dangerous pacifist and egalitarian ideas. Morihei himself avoided arrest, thanks to his contacts in the military and police establishments, but he remained under surveillance since he was considered "soft" by extremists. They did not like his stance that "*Bushido* is not learning how to die. *Bushido* is learning how to live, how to protect and foster life. Even in war, the taking of human life is to be avoided as much as possible. It is always a sin to kill. Give your opponents every chance to make peace." Morihei disliked teaching lethal techniques to members of the military and police academies, and he was dismayed when techniques he had taught showed up in military hand-to-hand combat manuals without his permission and without reference to *aiki*, disarming an attack nonviolently. The violence of war sickened Morihei. A disciple whose duties included giving Morihei a nightly massage became alarmed at how much thinner Morihei grew as the war dragged on.

Morihei's life was guided by visions. In December of 1940, Morihei had this vision:

> Around two o'clock in the morning as I was performing ritual purification, I suddenly forgot every martial art I had ever learned. All of the techniques handed down from my teachers appeared completely anew. Now they were vehicles for the cultivation of life, knowledge, virtue, and good sense, not devices to throw and pin people.

In 1942, an inner voice said to Morihei, "You are the one who must assume the mantle of the Prophet of Peace and teach human beings to live with creative courage. This is your calling, your privilege, your task. Go to the country, build a shrine dedicated to the Great Spirit of Peace and Harmony, and prepare yourself to be a guiding light for a new era." Morihei moved to Iwama, in Ibaraki Prefecture, to train, pray, and farm. Around this time, he began calling his teaching Aikido, which can be interpreted as "The Art of Peace."

The war came to a conclusion on August 15, 1945. Japan was in ruins, and the populace despondent, but Morihei was optimistic: "Instead of foolishly waging war, hereafter we will wage peace, the true purpose of Aikido. We will train to prevent war, to abolish nuclear weapons, to protect the environment, and to serve society." He told his handful of remaining students, "One day, this art will be practiced by people all over the world!"

When the war ended in 1945, Morihei's guru Onisaburo was cleared of all charges. Like Morihei, Onisaburo was supremely optimistic. Onisaburo passed the last two years of his life spreading his message of world peace and universal brotherhood. He said, "All I have ever wanted is world peace. Now that Japan has renounced war as part of its constitution, it will become a role model for the entire world." He was not worried about the American occupation of Japan. "The Americans will do a good job. The Japanese cannot reform themselves—they would be at each other's throats all the time." "Japan will recover economically," Onisaburo correctly predicted, but he added this warning to business people: "Don't get too greedy." Onisaburo also created a huge body of the most beautiful and delightful art—calligraphy, painting, and pottery—before he died. It is said that even on his deathbed he remained in typically high spirits.

In the years immediately following the end of the war, Morihei spent much of his time farming. He considered Aikido and farming to be an ideal combination, two activities that nourish both body and soul. There was also a severe food shortage at the time, and the farm at the Iwama *dojo* provided sustenance for a number of people. By the mid-1950s Japan had largely recovered from the aftermath of the war, and Aikido training was becoming well established both in Japan and abroad, due to the efforts of Morihei's son Kisshomaru (1912–1998) and other senior disciples. In the pre-war days, Morihei had been secretive with his techniques, never doing public demonstrations, and he had strictly limited the number of students he accepted, saying, "I want to keep an eye on everyone I teach." After the war he made a complete turnaround, becoming much more open, allowing himself to be freely photographed and filmed. He even appeared in two TV specials, one Japanese and one American—thus leaving us with a precious visual legacy. Morihei realized that people needed to see Aikido in the flesh, with their own eyes, and he became a tireless promoter of the Art of Peace. He also wanted to prove, through public demonstrations, that "this old fellow Morihei is still alive and kicking"—rumors had circulated after the war that the master had died. While female students were welcome from the start, Morihei initially opposed teaching Aikido to children because he felt that they were too young to understand the message. When Morihei saw how well children reacted and how much their parents appreciated the teaching, he relented. After a similar hesitation, he also approved the establishment of university Aikido clubs. The Aikido student base became much broader after these two changes.

Though he was rather stern and severe-looking in his forties and fifties, later in life Morihei seemed to be transfigured into the ideal image of a Taoist immortal: long, flowing white hair and a white beard, a serene countenance, sparkling eyes, and the most beatific of smiles. (In 1964, Morihei was informed that he would be presented with the Order of the Rising Sun from the emperor. He said to his students, "Perhaps I should shave my beard out of respect for his Imperial Highness." His students told him, "For us, your beard is part of our Aikido image. Please don't get rid of it." "I see," Morihei agreed. "The beard stays.") The writer C. W. Nicol, who did a lot of martial art training in his initial years in Japan, recalled, "To be in the same room with the *karate* master Masatatsu Oyama (1923–1994) [notorious for slaying bulls with his bare fists] was a frightening experience, but when I visited Ueshiba Sensei I felt nothing but warmth and light. Nonetheless, I still went flying when I tried to attack the Aikido master." A wrestler from Nepal came to see Morihei, and the master said, "Try to lift me." The wrestler could not budge Morihei and requested the secret of this technique. "I am one with the universe. Who can lift that?"

Once Morihei pinned a huge sumo wrestler named Mihamahiro with a single finger. This behemoth could lift hundreds of pounds, but when he tried to move Morihei, the diminutive master stayed firmly put. Morihei then threw Mihamahiro to the ground and held him immobile with a single finger. Morihei explained the feat like this: "Draw a circle around the center of a human being. Within this circle lies all physical power. Outside of this circle, even the strongest human being loses his power. If you can pin your partner outside of his sphere of strength, you can control him with just one finger."

Thus, Morihei taught that there was no need to build up enormous physical power. He said, "If you are strong enough to lift a suitcase you can practice Aikido." He told students further, "You fall down because I can walk." Nor was it necessary to attack an opponent's weak spots. "Disarm his aggressive spirit and he will naturally be subdued, without injury," Morihei explained.

Here are some remarks about Aikido from a talk Morihei gave to a group of college students in 1957:

Aikido is the Way of Harmony. It brings together people of all races and manifests the original form of all things. The universe has a single source, and from that core all things emerged in a cosmic pattern. At the end of WWII, it become clear that the world needed to be purified of filth and degradation, and that is why Aikido emerged. In order to eliminate war, deception, greed, and hatred, the gods of peace and harmony manifested their powers. All of us in this world are members of the same family, and we should work together to make discord and war disappear from our midst. Without Love, our nation, the world, and the universe will be destroyed. Love generates heat and light. Those two elements are actualized in physical form as Aikido. As the last aspect of creation, human beings came into existence as an actualization of all higher powers. Human beings represent all of creation and we must bring the divine plan to fruition. The purpose of education is to open your spirit. Modern education has forgotten this. The entire universe is a huge open book, full of miraculous things, and that is where true learning must be sought. In that spirit, take responsibility, train hard, develop yourselves, bloom in this world, and bear fruit.

Morihei enjoyed a wide circle of acquaintances, and there was a steady stream of visitors—royalty, politicians, religious leaders, business people, martial artists, athletes, Kabuki actors, Japanese dancers, scientists, movie stars—to his *dojo* in Tokyo. They all sought inspiration and often counsel as well. A well-known dance teacher from the Hanayanagi School always reviewed new dance routines with Morihei, asking for pointers on proper deportment and body movement. Morihei told a baseball player, "Do not try to guess how fast or slow a pitch will be. Just let the ball arrive at its own pace, and be there to greet it." He said to an actor, "Create your own universe and bring everything into your own sphere." Morihei was a great mystic but not antiscience. He would frequently ask people who he knew were industrial or medical researchers, "Any good inventions lately? If you apply the principles of Aikido to your work, some revolutionary new ideas are sure to pop up."

In general, Japanese martial artists tend to be conservative politically, often right-wing, even fascist in some extreme cases, but Morihei proclaimed Aikido to be the source of true democracy and real freedom. He told a member of the Japanese Communist Party, "I am a communist myself." "You are?" the startled comrade asked. "Yes, but my communist party is the one formed by the gods, not human beings. It is the communism of seeing all of humanity as comrades, as true equals, with equal access to the world's spiritual treasures."

While Morihei was personable and outgoing with his visitors, he was very strict with his disciples. He got angry if his students went around in untidy or disheveled training uniforms. He was constantly admonishing them for being inattentive when turning corners, climbing stairs, holding chopsticks, talking on the phone, riding on the subway, or for relying too much on flashlights in the dark. He told them that a real martial artist should be able to sense any threat that came within one hundred square meters of his person.

Morihei also played catch-me-if-you-can when traveling, typically disappearing into crowds, leaving one or two befuddled assistants trailing far behind. He once made a student retrace his steps across huge Ueno Station, telling him, "This time walk like a martial artist!" Some of his young disciples liked to show off, and one asked Morihei if he could use a live blade during a demonstration. "No," the master told him, "Better not." On another occasion, when Morihei was away, the student went ahead and used a live blade in a demonstration. Sure enough, he injured himself.

Morihei enjoyed testing his students in various ways. He could sense when a student was dozing off during one of his long lectures. He would call the startled student up to take breakfalls, and the student would then fall flat on his face because his legs had fallen asleep. In one instance, a strapping, young *judo* student petitioned Morihei to became a live-in disciple. Morihei put him on probation: he could watch the training, help cook the meals, and, in the evening, prepare the bath, massage Morihei's shoulders, and read bedtime stories to the master. Witnessing Morihei's daily routine and seemingly ordinary behavior, the student grew impatient and longed for the time when he could have a real go at his teacher. He spent most of his time silently plotting his attack. One day, Morihei suddenly announced, "Your training commences right now." The confident student leaped full force at Morihei, certain that he would get him; instead, he went flying several meters, landing hard on the mat. He was so stunned that afterward he was afraid to get near Morihei. He realized that he was the one who had been off guard the entire time, not the apparently nonchalant, totally at ease grandfather he had been serving, and thus he learned some valuable lessons—appearances are deceiving, and one's everyday deportment is the essence of martial art training.

Morihei's temper was explosive, but his outbursts cleared the air, and his anger quickly dissipated. Once, after the day's training had finished, Morihei heard a student yelling in the *dojo*. When Morihei walked in, he found the student swinging a wooden sword furiously, accompanied by guttural shouts. "What do you think you are doing?" Morihei reprimanded him. "Aikido is based on the projection of love. Why are you swinging that sword with such seething anger!"

Morihei also discouraged heavy drinking. After two of his senior students returned home from a night out on the town, he left them this note to ponder: "The ancient wise ones taught: 'Drinking liquor may make you feel spring in your heart, but it shuts off the path to enlightenment!'" Certain of Morihei's live-in disciples liked to sneak out at night, observing the utmost caution to cover their tracks. Despite their best *ninja*-like stealth, Morihei would invariably ask the next morning, "Did you fellows have a good time last night?" Or worse, he would show up for practice an hour early, rouse them from their drunken stupor, and conduct an extended and especially strenuous workout.

Once, the head instructor's valuable (and at the time very rare) leather jacket was stolen from the *dojo*. While he was berating the live-in disciples for their inexcusable inattentiveness, Morihei suddenly appeared in the *dojo*, asked what was going on, and, to everyone's surprise, instead reprimanded the head instructor, "It is your fault!" Morihei explained, "A martial artist should never be attached to material possessions or flaunt them openly. That kind of attitude creates openings in both in oneself and in others, and that is the reason such an event occurred." Sometimes Morihei was a kindly old sage, sometimes a strict mentor, and sometimes a fire-breathing god of wrath. A disciple described Morihei like this: "The Great Master is like Mount Fuji. So majestic and beautiful from a distance, so steep and dangerous to ascend when you get up close."

Morihei had a human side that was most apparent during his visit to Hawaii in 1961. At a reception in his honor, Morihei gleefully received a lei and the traditional kiss of greeting. He obviously took great delight in a hula performance by a beautiful young dancer, performed a dance with a fan and staff himself, and led the crowd in a rousing version of a Japanese folk song. Morihei could enjoy himself but remained the consummate martial artist at all times. As recounted in his memoirs, Roy Suenaga, a young Japanese American from Hawaii, was walking along the beach one night with Morihei when it occurred to him, "The master seems to be completely off his guard. I'm sure I could let him have it." Morihei stopped in his tracks, turned to him and said, "You shouldn't think like that. You need positive thoughts." When Suenaga dropped to his knees in apology, Morihei scolded him, "One simple apology is enough. Get up and don't do it again."

In a similar tale also set in Hawaii, a spectator was watching Morihei demonstrate movements against a sword attack. The spectator thought to himself, "He is only moving to one side. If I were up there, I would strike in that direction and nail him." After the demonstration, Morihei walked over to the man and announced with a smile, "That would not work either."

Morihei was asked if his miraculous powers were due to spirit possession. "No," the master replied. "The divine spirit is always present within me—and you too, if you delve deeply inside—so I am just obeying its commands and letting the awesome power of nature flow through me."

Morihei continued to train, travel, and teach widely until the very end. He said, "I do not need a *dojo* to practice Aikido. I'm not teaching for fame, status, or money. I can teach under a tree or on top of a rock. The entire world is my bridge to heaven. Ask and I will be glad to tell you about Aikido any time." In 1967, he fell ill with what was eventually diagnosed as terminal cancer, and grew very frail, but not weak. "When I do Aikido, old age and illness vanish!" he explained. One of his students described Morihei's invincible strength despite his illness:

Two of us disciples were attending the master on his deathbed one day when he told us, "I'm going to the *dojo*." He was not supposed to move around because of his frail condition, but there was no way for us to prevent him from doing what he wanted to do. We had to hold him as he walked to the *dojo* and carry him up the stairs, but as soon as he stepped onto the mat he straightened up and shrugged his shoulders, a simple movement that somehow sent both of us flying. The master placed himself before the *dojo* shrine and chanted for a few minutes. After that he trained with us briefly, bowed once more to the shrine, and sank back gently into our arms as we carried him out and returned him to his room.

Near the end, Morihei told a visitor, "I'm on a winged horse gazing down on the beautiful world below." He told his students, "Come join hands with this old grandpa to unite the world. We have no enemies in Aikido, none of us are strangers. Every day, let's train to make the world a little more peaceful." The last piece of calligraphy that Morihei brushed was *hikari*, or "light." Morihei said, "To me this world is a realm of light. Light illuminates all things. Sometimes that light is a fiery nimbus, sometimes a gentle radiance." Morihei died at dawn on April 26, 1969, at his home in Tokyo, at the age of eighty-six.

Students of Aikido revere Morihei as the Founder, the one who had the original vision of the Way of Harmony, the one who opened up this Path of Peace for us to follow. Morihei was a real flesh-and-blood human being who became a miracle-working prophet through constant forging of the body and life-long study of the spirit. Inspired by Morihei's example and his words, we train in Aikido, striving to reach a similar level of enlightenment.

Here are Morihei's Five Principles of Aikido, his last testament:

1. Aikido is the Great Path that traverses the universe and its domains. It encompasses and harmonizes all things.
2. Aikido functions in accordance with the truth received from heaven and earth. It should be the basis of all activity.
3. Aikido is the principle of unifying heaven, earth, and humankind.
4. Aikido allows each individual to follow a path suitable for him or her, enabling every human being to achieve harmony with the universe.
5. Aikido is the Way of supreme, unbounded, perfect, and inexhaustible Love that binds and sustains the universe.

_____

Hikari,
"light,"
Morihei's final piece of
calligraphy. His signature "Morihei" is to the
left, and beneath the charcacter is Morihei's
kao (personal cipher).

_Ai,_
the character for "love."

PART TWO

THE ART *of* WAR
versus
THE ART *of* PEACE

MORIHEI OFTEN SPOKE of the contrast between a material martial art and a spiritual martial art. (The Japanese words Morihei used were *haku* for "material" and *kon* for "spiritual.") He disliked the concept of "*Bushido*," or at least how it was interpreted by militarists. As mentioned earlier, Morihei taught that "*Bushido* is not learning how to die; it is learning how to live." He also criticized the warmongering of the *shoguns*: "There was nothing noble about using weapons and the arts of war to seize the land of other domains out of sheer greed." He decried false ideas of "honor," that led to ceaseless vendettas, and he was appalled by the once popular practice of *tsuji-giri* used by rogue samurai—deliberately provoking a fight to simply test the cutting power of a new blade.

Morihei described the difference between a material and a spiritual martial art:

> Material martial arts fixate on physical objects. That kind of martial art is a source of endless contention because it is based on the opposition of two forces. A spiritual martial art views things on a higher level. Its base is love, and it looks at things in their totality. It is formless, and never seeks to make enemies.

As seen in Morihei's biography in the first chapter, he had plenty of training in material martial arts, both Western and Japanese. This prophet of peace had been tested on many a battleground in real life, and he was hardly a dreamy idealist. In essence, Morihei became the ultimate martial artist by transcending the very concept of "martial art."

> People ask me, "Why is your *Budo* so different from all the other martial arts? Where did you learn this art of Aikido?"

I reply, "I studied various martial arts, but since they were all incomplete systems constructed by imperfect human beings, none of them provided me with a real answer to my question, 'What is the true purpose of *Budo*?' I had to find that truth myself, from within. In the past, martial arts were mistakenly believed to be a method of killing and snuffing out human life. Aikido, on the contrary, is a vehicle for preserving and fostering human life, a means of preventing murder and mayhem."

Morihei said further:

In order to establish heaven on earth, we need a *Budo* that is pure in spirit, that is devoid of hatred and greed. It must follow natural principles and harmonize the material with the spiritual. Aikido means not to kill. Although nearly all creeds have a commandment against taking life, most of them justify killing for one reason or another. In Aikido, however, we try to completely avoid killing, even of the most evil person.

Morihei disliked killing any living thing, even flies. His attitude was very similar to that of the great swordsman and Zen master Tesshu Yamaoka (1836–1888). In sharp contrast to the blood thirst of many martial artists, Tesshu was proud that he had never killed another human being despite being challenged by opponents armed to the teeth. (Like Morihei, Tesshu once walked unharmed right through a hail of bullets.) While the majority of martial artists in Japan take the ferocious, well-armed deity Fudo Myo-o as their patron saint, both Tesshu and Morihei preferred Kannon, the goddess of compassion. In fact, Morihei said that all the techniques of *Takemusu Aiki* were a means to manifest Kannon's works of mercy.

I have spent my life developing Aikido, and I still have a long way to go, but I know that it is a Way to promote love and goodness among humankind. While we should do nothing to sully the memory of the great masters of the past and we must be grateful for their legacy, we must build on their example to create a new *Budo* that follows the dictates of heaven, is free of shame, and continually manifests freshness and vitality. The world will continue to change dramatically, but fighting and war can destroy us utterly. What we need are techniques of harmony, not contention. The Art of Peace is required, not the Art of War.

Aikido is the *Budo* of the new millennium:

Aikido is the true martial art because it emerged from the truth of the universe. Since universal unity is at its center, Aikido sees everything in the cosmos as part of a single family, and it is an expression of ultimate harmony and absolute peace. Based on its universal vision, Aikido should be perceived as none other than the martial art of love. It can never be violent. Aikido is the embodiment of the Divine Creator, a truly august presence. Aikido is practiced at the junction of heaven and earth, in a peaceful manner. The purpose of Aikido is to teach people how not to be violent, and lead them to a higher path. It is a means of establishing universal peace. If we harmonize all nations together, there will be no need for atomic weapons, and this world will be a good and pleasant place to live.

There are no contests or organized competitions in Aikido because it is not a sport. Practitioners take turns being the "winner" and "loser" and try to cross the finish line hand in hand:

Sports are widely practiced nowadays, and they are good for physical exercise. In Aikido, too, we train the body but also use the body as a vehicle to train the mind, calm the spirit, and find goodness and beauty, dimensions that sports lack. Training in Aikido fosters valor, sincerity, fidelity, magnanimity, and beauty, as well as making the body strong and healthy. In Aikido, we train not to learn how to win; we train to learn to emerge victorious in any situation.

Morihei did speak of one kind of contesting for a great prize, however. He used the images of the Shinto creator deities Izanagi, or "He Who Invites," and Izanami, or "She Who Invites"—whose lovemaking gave birth to the world—to symbolize the irrepressible yearning for unity, the ceaseless striving to come together, that followers of Aikido should emulate as they seek to link themselves with the universe. Morihei also instructed his students to reflect deeply on the fusing of the two great creative powers of Male and Female, as represented by Izanagi and Izanami. Morihei's esoteric explanation of the stance used in Aikido is an example:

> Matter is female, a sword. Spirit is male, a spear. The left foot (leg) is male, and it stands in heaven. The right foot (leg) is female, and it stands on earth. Your body represents the central pillar of creation. The right foot is the base, the left foot responds in unlimited variations. Left represents *masakatsu* (true victory) and the male principle; right represents *agatsu* (self-victory) and the female principle; their integration is *katsuhayabi* (victory right here, right now), the birth of all techniques.

Morihei described Aikido techniques like this:

> All Aikido techniques must be linked to universal principles. Techniques that are not linked to higher principles will boomerang on you, and tear your body apart. In Aikido, change is the essence of technique. There are no forms in Aikido. Because there are no forms, Aikido is the study of the spirit. Do not get caught up in forms; if you do, you lose all the subtle distinctions that function in the techniques. In

Aikido, spiritual discernment is first, reformation of the heart second. A true technique is based on true thoughts. Use your body to manifest the spirit in physical form.

When instructing, in his later years, Morihei typically taught only basic techniques, and on occasion one of the younger and bolder students would complain, "Sensei, you have been doing the same technique for an hour. Please show us something different." "You idiot!" Morihei would exclaim. "Each and every one *was* different. When you can perceive the difference, that is when you will be making progress in Aikido." If someone asked to be shown a "secret technique," he would get a similar reply. "Each technique contains all the secrets you will ever need." Often, Morihei would then execute a technique called *tai-no-henko* (body turn), the simplest of all movements. Or he would say, "If you can do one good *shiho-nage* ["four-directions throw," a basic technique practiced every session] you will be close to mastering Aikido." If a student asked to see the footwork of a technique once more, Morihei would thunder, "I'm not teaching you how to move your feet; I'm teaching you how to move your mind!" Another student once said to Morihei, "When you are here with us in the *dojo* I can perform the techniques quite well, but when you are gone I cannot recall a thing." Morihei explained, "That is because I link your *ki* with mine and invisibly guide you. If you are ever in doubt or in trouble, think of me and I will assist you."

Much of Morihei's teaching was similar to that employed by Zen masters, who use koans, Zen puzzles, to keep their students on guard by giving them contradictory instructions. Morihei would tell certain students, "Aikido movements are all based on the sword; make the sword the basis of your training." Others, however, would be told the opposite: "Stay away from the sword until you learn how to use your body." Or "Never let your partner get a good grip on you," yet at the same time, "If you want to get strong, let your partner get a good grip and practice moving him." Regarding technique, Morihei made this telling remark:

> In reality, Aikido has no forms, no set patterns. It is like an invisible wave of energy. However, such a phenomenon is too difficult for human beings to grasp, so we use provisional forms to explain it and put it into practice. Any movement, in fact, can become an Aikido technique, so in ultimate terms, there are no mistakes. My advice to you: Learn and forget! Learn and forget! Make the techniques part of your being!

Similarly, if a student asked, "What is the name of that technique?" Morihei would reply, "Give it your own name. That will make it more personal." He further stated:

> You cannot imitate what I do. Each and every technique is a unique, once-and-for-all experience. My techniques emerge freely, spewing forth like a fountain. Rather than try to copy what I do, listen to what I say. That is where the essence of the techniques lies. Someday, you will understand.

_Yu,_
"Hidden"

Ai-ki-do,
the "Art of Peace,"
signed "Morihei."

PART THREE

THE ART *of* PEACE

The divine beauty

Of heaven and earth!

All creation,

Members of

One Family.

THE ART OF PEACE begins with you. Work on yourself and your appointed task in the Art of Peace. Everyone has a spirit that can be refined, a body that can be trained in some manner, a suitable path to follow. You are here for no other purpose than to realize your inner divinity and manifest your inner enlightenment. Foster peace in your own life and then apply the Art to all that you encounter.

•

One does not need buildings, money, power, or status to practice the Art of Peace. Heaven is right where you are standing, and that is the place to train.

•

All things, material and spiritual, originate from one source and are related as if they were one family. The past, present, and future are all contained in the life force. The universe emerged and developed from one source, and we evolved through the optimal process of unification and harmonization.

•

This is how the universe came into being: There was no heaven, no earth, no universe—just empty space. In this vast emptiness, a single point suddenly manifested itself. From that point, steam, smoke, and mist spiraled forth in a luminous sphere and the sacred sound SU was born. As SU expanded circularly up and down, left and right, nature and breath began,

The birth of the universe,
according to Aikido cosmology.
From the seed-symbol SU,
in the center, the sounds of
creation emerge in a circular
pattern: U-U-U-U-YU-MU.
Extending out from the
center are the sounds of
existence: A-O-U-E-I
(top to bottom).

clear and uncontaminated. Breath developed life, and sound appeared. SU is the Word mentioned in many world religions.

•

All sounds and vibrations emanate from that Word. Your voice is a very powerful weapon. When you are in tune with the cosmic breath of heaven and earth, your voice produces true sounds. Unify body, mind, and speech, and real techniques will emerge.

•

The Art of Peace emanated from the Divine Form and the Divine Heart of existence; it reflects the true, good, beautiful, and absolute nature of creation and the essence of its ultimate grand design. The purpose of the Art of Peace is to fashion sincere human beings; a sincere human being is one who has unified body and spirit, one who is free of hesitation or doubt, and one who understands the power of words.

•

Heaven, earth, humankind,
United in the Path of harmony and joy,
Following the Art of Peace,
Across the vast seas,
And on the highest peaks.

•

If you have life in you, you have access to the secrets of the ages, for the truth of the universe resides in each and every human being.

•

The Art of Peace is medicine for a sick world. We want to cure the world of the sickness of violence, malcontent, and discord—this is the Way of Harmony. There is evil and disorder in the world because people have forgotten that all things emanate from one source. Return to that source and leave behind all self-centered thoughts, petty desires, and anger. Those who are possessed by nothing possess everything.

•

Practice of the Art of Peace is an act of faith, a belief in the ultimate power of nonviolence. It is faith in the power of purification and faith in the power of life itself. It is not a type of rigid discipline or empty asceticism. It is a path that follows natural principles, principles that must be applied to daily living. The Art of Peace should be practiced from the time you rise to greet the morning to the time you retire at night.

•

Practice of the Art of Peace enables you to rise above praise or blame, and it frees you from attachment to this and that.

•

Shin,
"Divine."

Inner principles give coherence to things; the Art of Peace is a method of uncovering those principles.

●

A good mixture is 70 percent faith and 30 percent science. Faith in the Art of Peace will allow you to understand the intricacies of modern science.

●

Conflict between material and spiritual science creates physical and mental exhaustion, but when matter and spirit are harmonized, all stress and fatigue disappears.

●

Use your body to create forms; use your spirit to transcend forms; unify body and spirit to activate the Art of Peace.

●

If you have not
Linked yourself
To true emptiness,
You will never understand
The Art of Peace.

●

The Art of Peace functions everywhere on earth, in realms ranging from the vastness of space down to the tiniest plants and animals. The life force is all pervasive and its strength boundless. The Art of Peace allows us to perceive and tap into that tremendous reserve of universal energy.

●

Eight forces sustain creation:
Movement and stillness,
Solidification and fluidity,
Extension and contraction,
Unification and division.

●

Life is growth. If we stop growing, technically and spiritually, we are as good as dead. The Art of Peace is a celebration of the bonding of heaven, earth, and humankind. It is all that is true, good, and beautiful.

●

All things are bound together harmoniously; this is the real law of gravity that keeps the universe intact.

●

Now and again, it is necessary to seclude yourself among deep mountains and hidden valleys to restore your link to the source of life. Sit comfortably and first contemplate the manifest realm of existence. This realm is concerned with externals, the physical form of things. Then fill your body with *ki* and sense the manner in which the universe functions—its shape, its color, and its vibrations. Breathe in and let yourself soar to the ends of the universe; breathe out and bring the cosmos back inside. Next, breathe up all the fecundity and vibrancy of the earth. Finally, blend the breath of heaven and the breath of earth with that of your own body, becoming the breath of life itself. As you calm down, naturally let yourself settle in the heart of things. Find your center, and fill yourself with light and heat.

●

All the principles of heaven and earth are living inside you. Life itself is the truth, and this will never change. Everything in heaven and earth breathes. Breath is the thread that ties creation together. When the myriad variations in the universal breath can be sensed, the individual techniques of the Art of Peace are born.

●

Your breath is the true link to the universe. Ascending breath spirals upward to the right; descending breath spirals downward to the left. This interaction is the union of fire and water. It is the cosmic sound of A and UN, OM, *Alpha*, and *Omega*.

●

Consider the ebb and flow of the tide. When waves come to strike the shore, they crest and fall, creating a sound. Your breath should follow the same pattern, absorbing the entire universe in your belly with each inhalation. Know that we all have access to four treasures: the energy of the sun and moon, the breath of heaven, the breath of earth, and the ebb and flow of the tide.

●

Those who practice the Art of Peace must protect the domain of Mother Nature, the divine reflection of creation, and keep it lovely and fresh. Warriorship gives birth to natural beauty. The subtle techniques of a warrior arise as naturally as the appearance of spring, summer, autumn, and winter. Warriorship is none other than the vitality that sustains all life.

●

Life is a divine gift. The divine is not something outside of us; it is right in our very center; it is our freedom. In our training, we learn the real nature of life and death. When life is victorious, there is birth; when it is thwarted, there is death. A warrior is always engaged in a life-and-death struggle for peace.

●

Contemplate the workings of this world, listen to the words of the wise, and take all that is good as your own. With this as your base, open your own door to truth. Do not overlook the truth that is right before you.

●

Ikiru,
the character for "life."

True wisdom comes from intellectual education, physical education, ethical education, and *ki* education.

●

The universe is our greatest teacher, our greatest friend. It is always teaching us the Art of Peace. Study how water flows in a valley stream, smoothly and freely between the rocks. Everything—mountains, rivers, plants, and trees—should be your teacher. The world's wisdom is contained in books, and by studying the words of the wise, countless new techniques can be created. Study and practice, and then reflect on your progress. The Art of Peace is the art of learning deeply, the art of knowing oneself.

●

Create each day anew by clothing yourself with heaven and earth, bathing yourself with wisdom and love, and placing yourself in the heart of Mother Nature. Your body and mind will be gladdened, depression and heartache will dissipate, and you will be filled with gratitude.

●

Do not fail
To learn from
The pure voice of an
Ever-flowing mountain stream
Splashing over the rocks.

●

The Art of Peace originates with the flow of things—its heart is like the movement of the wind and waves. The Way is like the veins that circulate blood through our bodies, following the natural flow of the life force. If you are separated in the slightest from that divine essence, you are far off the path.

●

The Art of Peace possesses all wisdom and all power, and it gives birth to natural beauty. The subtle changes between the four seasons of spring, summer, autumn, and winter give birth to different techniques. The Art of Peace seeks to create ultimate beauty, a beauty that springs forth from the four corners and the eight directions of the world.

●

Your heart is full of fertile seeds, waiting to sprout. Just as a lotus flower springs from the mire to bloom splendidly, the interaction of the cosmic breath causes the flower of the spirit to bloom and bear fruit in this world.

●

Every sturdy tree that towers over human beings owes its existence to a deeply rooted core.

●

Study the teachings of the pine tree, the bamboo, and the plum blossom. The pine is evergreen, firmly rooted, and venerable. The bamboo is strong, resilient, unbreakable. The plum blossom is hardy, fragrant, and elegant.

●

Always keep your mind as bright and clear as the vast sky, the highest peak, and the deepest ocean, empty of all limiting thoughts.

●

In the Art of Peace you must be able to let yourself soar like a bird and sport like a whale.

●

Do not forget to pay your respect to the four directions each day. This wonderful world of ours is a creation of the divine, and for that gift we need to be ever grateful. That gratitude should be expressed through some kind of prayer. True prayer has no set form. Just offer your heartfelt gratitude in a way you feel is appropriate, and you will be amply rewarded.

●

Always keep your body filled with light and heat. Fill yourself with the power of wisdom and enlightenment.

Do (Tao),
the character for "way, path."

●

As soon as you concern yourself with the "good" and "bad" of your fellows, you create an opening in your heart for maliciousness to enter. Testing, competing with, and criticizing others weakens and defeats you.

●

The penetrating brilliance of swords
Wielded by followers of the Way
Strikes at the evil enemy
Lurking deep within
Their own souls and bodies.

●

In the Art of Peace, a single cut of the sword summons up the wondrous powers of the universe. That one sword links past, present, and future; it absorbs the universe. Time and space disappear. All of creation, from the distant past to the present moment, lives in this sword. All human existence flourishes right here in the sword you hold in your own hands. You are now prepared for anything that may arise.

●

Life is within death, death is within life; you must exist right here, right now!

Ten,
the character for
"heaven."

●

The delight of mountains, rivers, grasses, trees, beasts, fish, and insects is an expression of the Art of Peace.

●

The Art of Peace is not easy. It is a fight to the finish, the slaying of evil desires and all falsehood within. On occasion the voice of peace resounds like thunder, jolting human beings out of their stupor.

●

Crystal clear,
Sharp and bright,
The sacred sword
Allows no opening
For evil to roost.

●

To practice properly the Art of Peace, you must:

- Calm the spirit and return to the source.
- Cleanse the body and spirit by removing all malice, selfishness, and desire.
- Be ever grateful for the gifts received from the universe, your family, Mother Nature, and your fellow human beings.

●

The Art of Peace is based on the Four Great Virtues: Bravery, Wisdom, Love, and Friendship, symbolized by Fire, Heaven, Earth, and Water.

●

The essence of the Art of Peace is to cleanse yourself of maliciousness, to get in tune with your environment, and to clear your path of all obstacles and barriers.

●

The only real sin is to be ignorant of the universal, timeless principles of existence. Such ignorance is the root of all evil and all misguided behavior. Eliminate ignorance through the Art of Peace, and even hell will be emptied of tortured souls.

●

The only cure for materialism is the cleansing of the six senses (eyes, ears, nose, tongue, body, and mind). If the senses are clogged, one's perception is stifled. The more it is stifled, the more contaminated the senses become. This creates disorder in the world, and that is the greatest evil of all. Polish the heart, free the six senses and let them function without obstruction, and your entire body and soul will glow.

●

To purify yourself you must wash away all external defilements, remove all obstacles from your path, separate yourself from disorder, and abstain from negative thoughts. This will create a radiant state of being. Such purification allows you to return to the very beginning, where all is fresh, bright, and pristine, and you will see once again the world's scintillating beauty.

●

All life is a manifestation of the spirit, the manifestation of love. And the Art of Peace is the purest form of that principle. A warrior is charged with bringing a halt to all contention and strife. Universal love functions in many forms; each manifestation should be allowed free expression. The Art of Peace is true democracy.

●

Each and every master, regardless of the era or place, heard the call and attained harmony with heaven and earth. There are many paths leading to the peak of Mount Fuji, but the goal is the same. There are many methods of reaching the top, and they all bring us to the heights. There is no need to battle with each other—we are all brothers and sisters who should walk the Path together, hand in hand. Keep to your Path, and nothing else will matter. When you lose your desire for things that do not matter, you will be free.

●

Never fear another challenger, no matter how large;
Never despise another challenger, no matter how small.

●

Large does not always defeat little. Little can become large by constant building; large can become little by falling apart.

●

Loyalty and devotion lead to bravery. Bravery leads to the spirit of self-sacrifice. The spirit of self-sacrifice creates trust in the power of love.

●

Love is like the rays of the sun, shining left, right, up, down, front, back, bathing everything in light.

●

Economy is the basis of society. When the economy is stable, society develops. The ideal economy combines the spiritual and material, and the best commodities to trade in are sincerity and love.

●

The Art of Peace does not rely on weapons or brute force to succeed; instead, we put ourselves in tune with the universe, maintain peace in our own realms, nurture life, and prevent death and destruction. The true meaning of the term *samurai* is one who serves and adheres to the power of love.

•

Foster and polish
The warrior spirit
While serving in the world;
Illuminate the Path
According to your inner light.

•

The Path of Peace is exceedingly vast, reflecting the grand design of the hidden and manifest worlds. A warrior is a living shrine of the divine, one who serves that grand purpose.

•

Your mind should be in harmony with the functioning of the universe; your body should be in tune with the movement of the universe; body and mind should be bound as one, unified with the activity of the universe.

•

Even though our path is completely different from the warrior arts of the past, it is not necessary to abandon totally the old ways. Absorb venerable traditions into this new art by clothing them with fresh garments, and build on the classic styles to create better forms.

•

Daily training in the Art of Peace allows your inner divinity to shine brighter and brighter. Do not concern yourself with the right and wrong of others. Do not be calculating or act unnaturally. Keep your mind focused on the Art of Peace, and do not criticize other teachers or traditions. The Art of Peace never restrains or shackles anything. It embraces all and purifies everything.

•

Train hard, experience the light and warmth of the Art of Peace, and become a true person. Train more, and learn the principles of nature. The Art of Peace will be established all over, but it will have a different expression in each place it takes root. Continually adapt the teachings and create a beautiful environment.

•

In good training, we generate light (wisdom) and heat (compassion). Those two elements activate heaven and earth, the sun and moon; they are the subtle manifestations of water and fire. Unify the material and spiritual realms, and that will enable you to become truly brave, wise, loving, and empathetic.

Dai (okii),
the character for
"large, big, great."

•

Practice the Art of Peace sincerely, and evil thoughts and deeds will naturally disappear. The only desire that should remain is the thirst for more and more training in the Way.

•

Those who are enlightened never stop forging themselves. The realizations of such masters cannot be expressed well in words or by theories. The most perfect actions echo the patterns found in nature.

•

Day after day
Train your heart out,
Refining your technique:
Use the One to strike the Many!
That is the discipline of a Warrior.

•

Face a single foe as if you are facing ten thousand enemies; face ten thousand enemies as a single foe.

•

The Way of a Warrior
Cannot be encompassed

By words or in letters:
Grasp the essence
And move on toward realization!

●

The purpose of training is to tighten up the slack, toughen the body, and polish the spirit.

●

Iron is full of impurities that weaken it; through forging, it becomes steel and is transformed into a razor-sharp sword. Human beings develop in the same fashion.

●

From ancient times,
Deep learning and valor
Have been the two pillars of the Path:
Through the virtue of training,
Enlighten both body and soul.

●

Instructors can impart a fraction of the teaching. It is through your own devoted practice that the mysteries of the Art of Peace are brought to life.

●

The Way of a Warrior is based on humanity, love, and sincerity; the heart of martial valor is true bravery, wisdom, love, and friendship. Emphasis on the physical aspects of warriorship is futile, for the power of the body is always limited.

●

A true warrior is always armed with three things: the radiant sword of pacification; the mirror of bravery, wisdom, and friendship; and the precious jewel of enlightenment.

●

The heart of a human being is no different from the soul of heaven and earth. In your practice always keep in your thoughts the interaction of heaven and earth, water and fire, yin and yang.

●

The Art of Peace is the principle of nonresistance. Because it is nonresistant, it is victorious from the beginning. Those with evil intentions or contentious thoughts are vanquished. The Art of Peace is invincible because it contends with nothing.

●

There are no contests in the Art of Peace. A true warrior is invincible because he or she contests with nothing. Defeat means to defeat the mind of contention that we harbor within.

●

The Art of Peace is not an object that anyone possesses, nor is it something you can give to another. You must understand the Art of Peace from within, and express it in your own words.

●

To injure an opponent is to injure yourself. To control aggression without inflicting injury is the Art of Peace.

●

When your eyes engage those of another person, greet him or her with a smile and they will smile back. This is one of the essential techniques of the Art of Peace.

●

The totally awakened warrior can freely utilize all elements contained in heaven and earth. The true warrior learns how to correctly perceive the activity of the universe and how to transform martial techniques into vehicles of purity, goodness, and beauty. A warrior's mind and body must be permeated with enlightened wisdom and deep calm.

●

In the Art of Peace, we aim to see everything at once, taking in the entire field of vision in a single glance.

Ryu-o,
"Dragon king,"
Morihei's guardian angel.

●

Always practice the Art of Peace in a vibrant and joyful manner.

●

It is necessary to develop a strategy that utilizes all the physical conditions and elements that are directly at hand. The best strategy relies upon an unlimited set of responses.

●

In the Art of Peace, a technique can only work if it is in harmony with universal principles. Such principles need to be grasped though Mind, pure consciousness. Selfish desires thwart your progress, but Mind, not captivated by notions of victory or defeat, will liberate you. Mind fixes your senses and keeps you centered. Mind is the key to wondrous power and supreme clarity.

●

A good stance and posture reflect a proper state of mind.

●

The key to good technique is to keep your hands, feet, and hips straight and centered. If you are centered, you can move freely. Use this principle to guide your opponent and lead him (or her) in the direction that you want. If your opponent wants to pull, let him pull. Let him do whatever he wishes, and he will be unable to grasp on to anything to control.

●

The physical center is your belly; if your mind is set there as well, you are assured of victory in any endeavor.

●

Move like a beam of light:
Fly like lightning,
Strike like thunder,
Whirl in circles around
A stable center.

●

Techniques employ four qualities that reflect the nature of our world. Depending on the circumstance, you should be: hard as a diamond, flexible as a willow, smooth-flowing like water, or empty as space.

●

If your opponent strikes with fire, counter with water, becoming completely fluid and free-flowing. Water, by its nature, never collides with or breaks against anything. On the contrary, it swallows up any attack harmlessly.

●

Functioning harmoniously together, right and left give birth to all techniques. The left hand takes hold of life and death; the right hand controls it. The four limbs of the body are the four pillars of heaven, and manifest the eight directions, yin and yang, outer and inner.

●

Manifest yang
In your right hand,
Balance it with
The yin of your left,
And guide your partner.

●

The techniques of the Art of Peace are neither fast nor slow, nor are they inside or outside. They transcend time and space.

●

Spring forth from the Great Earth;
Billow like Great Waves;
Stand like a tree, sit like a rock;
Use the One to strike All.
Learn and forget!

●

The body should be triangular, the mind circular. The triangle represents the generation of energy and is the most stable physical posture. The circle symbolizes serenity and perfection, the source of unlimited techniques. The square stands for solidity, the basis of applied control.

●

Keep your movements circular. Imagine a circle with a cross drawn through it. Place yourself in the center and stand there confidently in a triangular stance. Link yourself to the *ki* of heaven and earth, pivot around the front foot, and guide your partner around that center.

●

You must be able to gauge the physical distance, the time distance, the psychological distance, and the energy distance between you and those who oppose you.

●

All of life is a circle, endlessly revolving, and that is the center point of the Art of Peace. The Art of Peace is a seamless, inexhaustible sphere that encompasses all things.

●

Always try to be in communion with heaven and earth; then the world will appear in its true light. Self-conceit will vanish, and you can blend with any attack.

Waza,
the character for
"technique."

●

There is no place in the Art of Peace for pettiness and selfish thoughts. Rather than being captivated by the notion of "winning or losing," seek the true nature of things. Your thoughts should reflect the grandeur of the universe, a realm beyond life and death. If your thoughts are antagonistic toward the cosmos, those thoughts will destroy you and wreak havoc on the environment.

●

If your heart is large enough to envelop your adversaries, you can see right through their petty mindedness and avoid their attacks. And once you envelop them, you will be able to guide them along a path indicated to you by heaven and earth.

●

Free of weakness,
No-mindedly ignore
The sharp attacks
Of your enemies:
Step in and act!

●

Do not look upon this world with fear and loathing. Bravely face whatever the gods offer.

●

Each day of human life contains joy and anger, pain and pleasure, darkness and light, growth and decay. Each moment is etched with nature's grand design—do not try to deny or oppose the cosmic order of things.

●

Protectors of this world
And guardians of the Ways
Of gods and buddhas,
The techniques of peace
Enable us to meet every challenge.

●

Life itself is always a trial. In training, you must test and polish yourself in order to face the great challenges of life. Transcend the realm of life and death, and then you will be able to make your way calmly and safely through any crisis that confronts you.

●

Face any challenge head-on. When an attack comes head-on, employ the principle of "moon reflected on the water." The moon appears to be really present, but if you strike the water, nothing will be there. Similarly, your opponent should find nothing solid to strike. Like the moonlight, envelop your opponent, physically and spiritually, until there is no separation between you.

●

Attacks can come from any direction—from above, from the middle, from below; from the front, from the back; from the left, from the right. Keep centered and remain unshakable.

●

Be grateful even for hardship, setbacks, and bad people. Dealing with such obstacles is an essential part of training in the Art of Peace.

●

The divine never condemns any human being as totally bad. The divine wants evildoers to realize the folly of their actions from within; then they will joyfully mend their pernicious ways. Give misguided souls a good example, and they will become aware of what a great wonder life is, and naturally reform.

●

Failure is the key to success;
Each mistake teaches us something.

_____

Hi,
the character for
"day, time, sun,"
and the
seed-syllable "SU."

●

In extreme situations, the entire universe becomes our foe; at such critical times, unity of mind and technique is essential— do not let your heart waver!

●

In order to practice the Art of Peace, we need valor, a valor that is grounded in truth, goodness, and beauty. Valor gives us strength and makes us brave. Valor is a mirror that reveals all things and exposes evil.

●

At the instant
A warrior
Confronts a foe,
All things
Come into focus.

●

Even when called out
By a single foe,
Remain on guard,
For you are always surrounded
By a host of enemies.

●

Do not hope
To avoid a thrust
When it comes;
Disarm it
Right at the source!

•

No matter how heavily armed your opponent is, you can use the Art of Peace to disarm him (or her). When someone comes in anger, greet him with a smile. That is the highest kind of martial art.

•

When someone stands in opposition to you, there is an even, fifty-fifty split. Greet an opponent who comes forward; bid goodbye to an opponent who withdraws. Keep the original balance and your opponent will have nowhere to strike. In fact, your opponent is not really your opponent because you and your opponent become one. This is the beauty of the Art of Peace.

•

The Art of Peace is to fulfill that which is lacking.

•

One should be prepared to receive 99 percent of an enemy's attack and stare death right in the face in order to illumine the

Path. Regardless of how grim a situation, it is still possible to turn things around in your favor.

●

In our techniques we enter completely into, blend totally with, and control firmly an attack. Strength resides where one's *ki* is concentrated and stable; confusion and maliciousness arise when *ki* stagnates.

●

There are two types of *ki*: ordinary *ki* and true *ki*. Ordinary *ki* is coarse and heavy; true *ki* is light and versatile. In order to perform well, you have to liberate yourself from ordinary *ki* and permeate your organs with true *ki*. That is the basis of powerful technique. *Ki* can be a gentle breeze rustling the leaves, or a fierce wind snapping large branches.

●

In the Art of Peace we never attack. An attack is proof that one is out of control. Never run away from any kind of challenge, but do not try to suppress or control an opponent unnaturally. Let attackers come any way they like and then blend with them. Never chase after opponents. Redirect each attack and get firmly behind it.

●

Seeing me before him,
The enemy attacks,
But by that time
I am already standing
Safely behind him.

●

When attacked, unify the upper, middle, and lower parts of
your body. Enter, turn, and blend with your opponent, front and
back, right and left.

●

Ancient warriors used pillars and trees as shields, but that will
not do. Nor can you rely on others to protect you. Your spirit is
the true shield.

●

Opponents confront us continually, but actually there is no opponent there. Enter deeply into an attack and neutralize it as
you draw that misdirected force into your own sphere.

●

Do not stare into the eyes of your opponent: he may mesmer-
ize you. Do not fix your gaze on his sword: he may intimidate
you. Do not focus on your opponent at all: he may absorb your

Take (bu),
the character for
"martial, valor, courage."

energy. The essence of training is to bring your opponent completely into your sphere. Then you can stand just where you like.

●

Even the most powerful human being has a limited sphere of strength. Draw him outside of that sphere and into your own, and his strength will dissipate.

●

Left and right,
Avoid all
Cuts and parries.
Seize your opponents' minds
And scatter them all!

●

The real Art of Peace is not to sacrifice a single one of your warriors to defeat an enemy. Vanquish your foes by always keeping yourself in a safe and unassailable position; then no one will suffer any losses. The Way of a Warrior, the Art of Politics, is to stop trouble before it starts. It consists in defeating your adversaries spiritually by making them realize the folly of their actions. The Way of a Warrior is to establish harmony.

●

Master the divine techniques
Of the Art of Peace,
And no enemy
Will dare to
Challenge you.

•

In your training, do not be in a hurry, for it takes a minimum
of ten years to master the basics and advance to the first rung.
Never think of yourself as an all-knowing, perfected master;
you must continue to train daily with your friends and students
and progress together in the Art of Peace.

•

Progress comes
To those who
Train and train;
Reliance on secret techniques
Will get you nowhere.

•

Fiddling with this
And that technique
Is of no avail.
Simply act decisively
Without reserve!

•

Ki,
the character for
"vital energy."

To learn how to
Discern the rhythm
Of strikes and thrusts
Stick to the basics—
The secrets are on the surface!

●

If you perceive the true form of heaven and earth, you will be enlightened to your own true form. If you are enlightened about a certain principle, you can put it into practice. After each practical application, reflect on your efforts. Progress continually like this.

●

The heart of the Art of Peace is: *True Victory is Self-Victory; Day of Swift Victory!* "True Victory" means unflinching courage; "Self-Victory" symbolizes unflagging effort; and "Day of Swift Victory" represents the glorious moment of triumph in the here and now. The Art of Peace is free of set forms, so it responds immediately to any contingency, which thus assures us of true victory; it is invincible because it contends with nothing. Rely on *True Victory is Self-victory, Day of Swift Victory* and you will be able to integrate the inner and outer factors of life, clear your path of obstacles, and cleanse your senses.

●

Victory over oneself is the primary goal of our training. We focus on the spirit rather than the form, the kernel rather than the shell.

•

Cast off limiting thoughts and return to true emptiness. Stand in the midst of the great void. This is the secret of the Way of a Warrior.

•

To truly implement the Art of Peace, you must be able to sport freely in the manifest, hidden, and divine realms.

•

If you comprehend
The Art of Peace,
This difficult path,
Just as it is,
Envelops the circle of heaven.

•

The techniques of the Way of Peace change constantly; every encounter is unique, and the appropriate response should emerge naturally. Today's techniques will be different tomorrow. Do not get caught up with the form and appearance of a challenge. The Art of Peace has no form—it is the study of the spirit.

•

Ultimately, you must forget about technique. The further you progress, the fewer teachings there are. The Great Path is really No Path.

•

Fathom the essences of the Art of Peace and age disappears. You only feel old when you lose your way and stray from the path.

•

The Art of Peace that I practice has room for each of the world's eight million gods, and I cooperate with them all. The God of Peace is very great and enjoins all that is divine and enlightened in every land.

•

The Art of Peace is a form of prayer that generates light and heat. Forget about your little self, detach yourself from objects, and you will radiate light and warmth. Light is wisdom; warmth is compassion.

•

We can no longer rely on the external teachings of Buddha, Confucius, or Christ. The era of organized religion controlling every aspect of life is over. No single religion has all the answers. Construction of shrine and temple buildings is not enough. Establish yourself as a living buddha image. We all should be transformed into goddesses of compassion or victorious buddhas.

Kami,
the character for "divine."

•

Rely on Peace
To activate your
Manifold powers;
Pacify your environment
And create a beautiful world.

•

The divine is not something high above us. It is in heaven, it is in earth, it is inside us.

•

Unite yourself to the cosmos, and the thought of transcendence will disappear. Transcendence belongs to the profane world. When all trace of transcendence vanishes, the true person—the divine being—is manifest. Empty yourself and let the divine function.

•

You cannot see or touch the divine with your gross senses. The divine is within you, not somewhere else. Unite yourself to the divine, and you will be able to perceive gods wherever you are, but do not try to grasp or cling to them.

•

The divine does not like to be shut up in a building. The divine likes to be out in the open. It is right here in this very body. Each one of us is a miniature universe, a living shrine.

•

When you bow deeply to the universe, it bows back; when you call out the name of God, it echoes inside you.

•

The Art of Peace is the religion that is not a religion; it perfects and completes all religions.

•

The Path is exceedingly vast. From ancient times to the present day, even the greatest sages were unable to perceive and comprehend the entire truth; the explanation and teachings of masters and saints express only part of the whole. It is not possible for anyone to speak of such things in their entirety. Just head for the light and heat, learn from the gods, and through the virtue of devoted practice of the Art of Peace, become one with the divine.

•

Unification of body and spirit through the Art of Peace is an exalted state, so high and pleasant that it brings tears of joy to your eyes.

Aiki okami,
"Great Spirit of Aikido,"
signed "Tsunemori."